CROSSING CULTURES

Also available in the Pioneer *Perspectives* series:

Better Than or Equal To?	Linda Harding
Caring for New Christians	Margaret Ellis
Christian Citizenship	Mike Morris
Healing Then and Now	Martin Scott
Prophecy in the Church	Martin Scott
Radical Evangelism	Pete Gilbert
Relationships—Jesus Style	Stuart Lindsell
The Power to Persuade	Cleland Thom
The Role and Ministry of Women	Martin Scott
The Worshipping Church	Noel Richards
Your Mind Matters	Chris Seaton

For further information on the Pioneer *Perspectives* series and Pioneer, please write to:

P.O. Box 79c, Esher, Surrey, KT10 9LP

CROSSING CULTURES

Building Bridges in Mission

Paul Dakin

WORD PUBLISHING
Nelson Word Ltd
Milton Keynes, England

WORD AUSTRALIA
Kilsyth, Victoria, Australia

NELSON WORD CANADA
Vancouver, B.C., Canada

STRUIK CHRISTIAN BOOKS (PTY) LTD
Cape Town, South Africa

JOINT DISTRIBUTORS SINGAPORE—
ALBY COMMERCIAL ENTERPRISES PTE LTD
and
CAMPUS CRUSADE, ASIA LTD

PHILIPPINE CAMPUS CRUSADE FOR CHRIST
Quezon City, Philippines

CHRISTIAN MARKETING NEW ZEALAND LTD
Havelock North, New Zealand

JENSCO LTD
Hong Kong

SALVATION BOOK CENTRE
Malaysia

CROSSING CULTURES

Published by Nelson Word Ltd. / Pioneer 1994.

ISBN 0-85009-736-3

Front cover illustration: *The Boat During the Flood at Port-Marly,* Alfred Sisley, courtesy of Musée d'Orsay, Paris. Giraudon/Bridgeman Art Library (detail).

Reproduced, printed and bound in Great Britain for Nelson Word Ltd. by Cox and Wyman Ltd., Reading.

94 95 96 97 / 10 9 8 7 6 5 4 3 2 1

FOREWORD

Pioneer *Perspectives* are perhaps more than their title suggests!

They are carefully researched presentations of material, on important issues, appealing to thinking churches, creative leaders and responsible Christians.

Each *Perspective* pioneers in as much as it is at the cutting edge of biblical and theological issues. Each will continue to pioneer with new ideas, concepts and data drawn from Scripture, history and a contemporary understanding of both.

They are perspectives in as much as they aim to be an important contribution to the ongoing debate on issues such as women in ministry and leadership; prophets and prophecy in the church; biblical models of evangelism; integrating and discipling new believers; growing and building local churches and further perspectives on Christ's second coming.

Importantly, these studies use a journal style of presentation, and are written by people who are currently working out the implications of the issues they are writing about, in local churches. This is vital if we are to escape the dangerous fantasy of abstract theology without practical experience. They are not written to contribute to the paralysis of analysis—rather to feed, strengthen, nurture and inform so that we can be equipped to get God's will done, by networking the nations with the gospel using all the resources that are available to us.

God's Word is always an event. How much we thank Him that He has left us an orderly account of what He wants us to believe, how He wants us to live, and what He wants us to do in order to bring heaven to the earth. As we embrace a better understanding of Scripture, rooted in local church, national and international mission, we shall become a part of the great eschatological purpose of bringing back the King—not for a church defeated, cowering and retiring but for one which, despite colossal odds, pressures and persecutions, is faithful to her Lord and His Word. To do that we must 'search the Scriptures' to see if many of these 'new things' are true. I commend these *Perspectives* to you as they are published on a regular basis throughout these coming years.

Gerald Coates
Director Pioneer Trust/Team Leader

Pioneer consists of a team and network of churches, committed to dynamic and effective biblical Christianity.

The national team act as advisers and consultants to churches, which in many cases develop into a partnership with the Pioneer team. These are the churches keen to identify with the theology, philosophy, ethos and purpose of Pioneer. The team have a vigorous youth ministry, church-planting strategy and evangelistic emphasis.

Training courses include Equipped to Lead, Emerging Leaders and the highly successful TIE teams (Training In Evangelism).

Pioneer have also been instrumental in initiating and funding March for Jesus (with Ichthus/YWAM); Jubilee Campaign (for the suffering church worldwide); and ACET (Aids Care Education Training).

CONTENTS

INTRODUCTION 11

CHAPTER 1 : The Meaning of Culture 17

CHAPTER 2 : Reaching the World 25

CHAPTER 3 : Crossing Cultures in the Old Testament 33

CHAPTER 4 : Jesus—the Cross-cultural Life 41

CHAPTER 5 : Crossing Cultures in the New Testament 47

CHAPTER 6 : Culture in the Church 57

CHAPTER 7 : UK Culture 65

CHAPTER 8 : Crossing the Divide 73

CHAPTER 9 : Seizing the Time 81

CHAPTER 10 : Integrated Church 89

RECOMMENDED READING 93

INTRODUCTION

Dusk was falling rapidly. Some of the market traders were starting to light fires as they finished the day's work. As I turned to pay the driver of the motorised rickshaw, the unfamiliar sounds and smells engulfed me.

I had been working within this non-stop, sprawling Asian nation for some weeks, and prided myself on my ability to travel around without the customary Western panic so easily seen in the rare tourists. As I looked about, a surprising coldness filled the depths of my stomach. For a moment, I felt giddy in the half-light.

Some minutes before, I had left one part of this city, having arranged to follow my wife and a friend who travelled in the 'autorick' ahead. They could only take two passengers. When I had ordered the driver to take me to the City Garage, it was in the naive belief that there was only one central bus depot in the city. At least, I had only ever been to one.

As he accelerated away, having supposedly dropped me at the agreed destination, I could feel the sense of horror strike from within. The realisation dawned upon me that I was hopelessly lost. I had parted with the only money in my pocket, but I had no idea of where I was. There were no maps, no telephones, only a sea of curious faces with whom I quickly established no conversation was possible. My natural fluency in English was utterly useless amidst the insistent and unintelligible sounds of Telugu, Tamil, Kannada and Urdu.

Pictures flashed through my mind: my wife and friend arriving at our agreed destination, only to discover that I was missing. I was unable to do anything that might allay their fears. I recalled the occasion when I was only four, getting lost on the promenade at Cleethorpes. At least there, I had been able to gain the sympathy and friendly ear of an elderly man. He had found a nearby policeman who took me hand in hand to the Lost Property office on the beach, where my father eventually found me! The shame associated with that early brush with what seemed like a very long arm of the Law was a gentle emotion compared with the fear that gripped me now.

My whole appearance attracted attention. It was unusual to see Westerners in the city anyway, but especially in this rundown section of town. Because we had been out visiting, I was wearing white clothes and carrying a camera. I was so obviously different, and so clearly lost. It was as if time stood still, and everything that was comfortable and familiar seemed so impossibly beyond reach.

Somehow I was able to start thinking straight. I tried to come up with a point of reference known to myself and the people in the market. Remembering the name of the main railway station, I started bellowing those words to the faces around me. Even though that English phrase was used by people, I discovered that my pronunciation was not understood. Eventually, by using actions as well as words, we managed to find some mutual point of recognition. Instantly, as the gathering crowd realised what I was looking for, a forest of hands shot out pointing the way to the station. Unfortunately, they were all aiming in different directions!

After renewed discussion among the onlookers, a consensus of opinion emerged, and I set off in the hope that this was the general direction of my destination. It was not long before I wished that I was somewhere else. I had turned into a tightly packed street filled with shops in a neighbourhood that was obviously poor, even for this city. I could not have felt more conspicuous, with my dress, appearance, manner and language completely alien to the setting. It seemed as if every man, woman and child stopped talking and stared. The mass of people parted in front of me as I passed along.

Alone and friendless, with no guarantee that the station was ahead, I began to look about me with suspicion, misreading any casual movement as a threat.

After what seemed to be hours of walking, I reached a crossroads and had no idea of which way to turn. There were no familiar faces, no recognisable signs or sites. In desperation, I stopped at the side of the road and looked upwards to pray. What a strange sight that must have been! Having fervently asked God to do something, anything, I caught sight of a uniformed figure appearing around the corner—a policeman! It is true that he bore little similarity to the comforting, homely vision of a British bobby, but his arrival was nonetheless welcome! He was astonished to find me rushing across the street asking for directions, but fortunately his knowledge of English was good enough to assure me of the way I needed.

Striding confidently away, it did not seem long before I saw the reassuring sight of the familiar bus depot. No weary traveller could ever have been so relieved to plunge into the throng of rickety buses and rushing humanity! How my spirits soared to be back on well-known territory! Within a short time I had found my wife and friend, who had become more and more convinced that I had been kidnapped. Everybody stopped and stared as we shrieked and embraced, not stopping to consider that such actions were culturally unacceptable.

Some weeks before, on my arrival in this country, I had spent several days experiencing 'culture shock'. The people who had organised my stay had warned me of this phenomenon which occurs when travelling to a very different society. Being bombarded by a different set of sounds, sights and smells can be disorientating, when we discover that speech, dress, manners and mindset may not fit into the neat little boxes with which we have grown used to handling the information presented by the world around us. It takes time to adjust to the new pace and ways of living, and to find points of reference to make us feel secure. The long-term goals of learning culture and language require persistence and commitment, and can only be reached gradually over the years.

The unfortunate experience that I have described above is an example not so much of 'culture shock' but more of 'culture terror'! Looking back, I can see that so much of what I felt during that episode was a concentrated, heightened version of a similar process that affects a great many people today. We do not have to go abroad to find many individuals suffering because of a mismatch between their own background, upbringing and experience and the prejudices and expectations of those around them.

Reducing this story to basic principles, we find that there are a number of features common to any situation where people are overwhelmed by the different perceptions that they may have from those around them:

- loss of the familiar
- strange locations
- separation from family/friends
- mistaken expectations
- inability to communicate
- difficulties with money
- inappropriate dress/appearance
- behaviour interpreted differently
- racial difference
- social difference

It is simple to see how this could be reproduced in any part of the UK, when contact is made between individuals of dissimilar background. This is seen most clearly with people from another country or ethnic group, but may also be seen, perhaps more subtly, in the mix of other social groupings based around class and background.

As a result, a whole range of disturbances can be produced at the time of this contact, the effects of which are to prevent rather than improve communication:

- fear
- anxiety
- mistrust
- confusion
- suspicion
- prejudice
- desperation

The intention of this book is to encourage God's people to communicate the reality of Jesus to all people, despite the fascinating array of variation in humankind. This is done in the belief that God wants the good news about His desire for relationship with Him to reach every people group across the face of the earth, in order to see the return of the King.

Without realising it, we may put obstacles in the way of effective communication, simply because of who we are and the way we do things. What we may take for granted from our background, and what seems appropriate for us, may not be as obvious or as important for one who does not share that same set of perceptions.

We cannot wholly separate out the message and the messenger. Indeed it would not be helpful if we could. The world needs to see that we *are* the good news, as well as *speaking* the good news. However, it is important to make our evangelism sensitive and wise in order to spread the gospel, rather than get nowhere simply because our approach is relevant only to other people who are cast in the same mould as ourselves.

God is looking for a generation that will emphasise the common needs of all people groups as well as take pleasure in their differences. He is looking for a church that is ready to build bridges between communities, and to take on the task of culturally relevant mission.

CHAPTER 1

THE MEANING OF CULTURE

The idea of 'culture' is often associated with a rather refined, snobbish taste which is inaccessible to most people. The enjoyment of opera, art galleries and ballet would represent such a largely inaccurate but popular view. This may characterise one meaning of the word, but the whole concept is much more fundamental and touches us all.

The world is full of a tremendous variety of people, of whom no two are identical. There are many underlying similarities, but also a great many differences which help us to distinguish one person from another. This vast array of characteristics ranges from the obvious to the subtle. Size, shape, hair colour, sound of voice are some. Other influential characteristics are not readily seen, such as language, education, religion.

When we try to describe a population of people, we can define some of these given areas such as race, nationality and ethnic origin. However, within these large culture groups are many others which may not be so easily identifiable as groups. We may recognise particular trends, ideas and behaviour patterns which in turn can overlap or transcend larger ethnic or language considerations.

Definition

Culture involves the whole of human creation. It constitutes the way of life of an entire society, or a specific group within it. It includes codes of manners, dress, language and rituals. Culture is expressed through norms of behaviour which are linked to an underlying system of values and beliefs.

Norms are defined as concrete ways of feeling, thinking and acting which reflect a set of beliefs. Values tend to be more abstract, and are the collective beliefs of that group.

These are common to those within that culture, but may not be easily understood or can be interpreted differently by those who are outside it. Indeed the same words, symbols or behaviour may have different meanings in different cultures. For instance, what is acceptable in terms of dress, hair length and physical contact can vary tremendously from one group to another.

Culture is a framework around which patterns of behaviour and communication are possible. Every day, we take for granted that ideas which we have in our minds can be transformed into speech in order to express the same concept accurately in the understanding of someone else. The use of symbols is particularly important.

Symbols

In trying to communicate with one another, we use symbols which are often a form of 'shorthand', and expressions of speech which save time. This is true in a 'Christian' culture. We speak of the symbol of a cross which may convey a vast wealth of emotion and information to another believer. To an outsider, the relevance of two pieces of wood may not be obvious. What they can actually see is only a small part of the meaning of that particular symbol.

Some years ago, I was leading a home group. In those days, many of us did not see the need to speak in a language or with ideas that people outside the Christian community could understand. One of my friends brought his neighbour, who had recently left the Navy. Halfway through the evening, as we were in full theological flight, he stopped us all by asking, 'When you talk about God, what exactly do you mean?'

Our most familiar ideas may not be clear even within our own circle. Current UK society is losing its Christian heritage. As a result, there are increasing numbers of people who have never come across the concepts and symbols which are so important to Christian belief. To gain access to any culture it is necessary to have enough information about it to understand the symbols used.

Language

Whenever we communicate any idea or truth, it is expressed in language and clothed with culture. This is obvious in terms of the different languages and idioms used by separate ethnic groups. As we shall see in a later chapter, there is an exciting and extensive mix of tongues spoken within the UK. One of the challenges of modern mission at home and abroad is to convey concepts across the divides of language and background.

Sometimes the idea we try to convey is unfamiliar to the people with whom we are sharing the gospel. I was asked to speak to the leaders of a church in Devon about scriptural principles in leadership. When discussing the apostolic role, I used the outdated and, as it turned out, unfortunate word 'covering'. I noticed that every time this word was used, there were one or two odd glances. Nothing further was said until the very end of the meeting. As he was leaving, an older farmer took me to one side and said, 'You've never worked on a farm, have you?'

I readily admitted that this was true.

He smiled and continued, 'If you had, you wouldn't have kept talking about "covering".'

Somewhat perplexed, I asked him why not.

The old man said, 'Let's put it this way. Suppose you

wanted to add to your herd of cattle. You would leave a cow in a field and introduce it to a bull. When the bull did what you hoped it would—that is covering!'

That night my Christian vocabulary had a word deleted!

Identity

Any society consists of a series of social groups or people groups which are based around certain well-defined characteristics. These are taken for granted within the group, and act to give it an identity. This identity is passed on to those who are part of the group and who want to ascribe to that set of common shared values. The culture, however it is expressed, gives a sense of purpose and meaning, a framework from which to relate to the world and events that take place. There is an *inclusive* feel about it.

However, the same values that serve to integrate a group also prevent others from entering it. Culture is *exclusive* as well, to those who do not share the same norms and background. For instance, one style of music may appeal to one group more than to another, and it may be valid to use this in an attempt to bridge the gap.

Identity is developed through a common background such as a place of origin or way of speaking. It can be maintained through shared knowledge which builds a tradition. It can happen because of shared experience, as with music, dress and behaviour. Any group which has similarities seen from both inside and outside can be termed 'homogeneous'.

Resistance to change

Generally speaking, much within culture is difficult to change rapidly. Because of the support which a common identity brings, there is comfort for most people in keeping things as they are rather than risking any fundamental change. It is interesting to see how strongly these values are held. I once worked with an Armenian. Although he stated that he was an atheist, he told me with great pride that he would willingly die for the Christian tradition because it was a cornerstone of his national heritage. He had no personal investment in the beliefs, but gained a tremendously strong sense of history and identity from them.

To ignore the power and effect of culture on the actions of individuals can be dangerous. Recently we have seen the re-emergence of hidden cultural differences which had been suppressed within living memory. The older 'tribal' differences which preceded the Communist system have woken once more. People who have been educated in an egalitarian, nonreligious system are fighting for a culture which places a priority on history and race. The old Yugoslavia and Soviet Union are fermenting with the brutal expression of ethnic, religious and cultural divides.

I trained with a young man from one of the 'closed' Muslim countries. In fact his father was a government minister. We often used to talk about the Bible and the Qur'an, and in many ways he was the most non-Arab Arab that I have ever met. He seemed so Western in his approach to every aspect of life. I remember the day his wife had their first child. They were both so excited and had said they were just interested in a healthy baby, whatever the sex. That is, until his wife had a beautiful, bouncing baby girl. For three hours, my friend ranted and raved around the labour ward. His wife had failed him by producing a first-born girl, not a boy. For a short while the Western veneer was stripped away and we were confronted with the desert traditions of a thousand years. Eventually he settled down and accepted his daughter for the lovely child that she was. The effects of our background, upbringing and culture upon us can be greater than we realise.

Relevant culture

It is in the enemy's interest to keep people apart. Any difference between sections of humanity can be used to create barriers, preventing meaningful contact and understanding. The enemy knows that if communication occurs across these potential divisions, the gospel will spread. He is implacably opposed to this process, as it is the extension of the truth about Jesus that will bring about his downfall.

All truth and belief are clothed in cultural form. We cannot avoid this. Indeed this is not unhealthy. What is important to us becomes expressed in ways that are appropriate and accessible.

There is nothing wrong in us owning our background and a particular approach that works for us. The drawback is in believing that what works for us will work for everyone else *regardless of their background.* If we are to share the gospel with those of another cultural group we need to put their need to hear ahead of our desire to be comfortable. The truth that we wish to share is the same for us all and just as relevant. However, the way in which we communicate it needs to be accessible and appropriate.

I once visited a church in a Moroccan city. Morocco has a small number of Christians and desperately needs to hear and respond to the reality of Jesus. The small congregation had only one man who was not a foreign exile. This was hardly surprising as the style of the building, worship and relationships were clearly an export of the English parish church. How anyone could imagine that this would ever be relevant to a North African Muslim society was beyond me.

In another country the local Christians were marked out by the fact that they wore shoes in place of the local sandals, and shirts and ties instead of dhotis. Even the church services were in English although the majority of the local population could not speak it. Christian teaching seemed only to be available to those who had enough money and sufficient education.

It is easy for us to be trapped within our own culture, unable to break out into evangelising any group that does not share the same background or approach. This would be of little importance in an area where people are all part of a homogeneous group. However, there are few, if any, areas even of this nation where that would be true. There are now so many people groups of one form or another that we need to be prepared to cross cultures.

CHAPTER 2

REACHING THE WORLD

At the heart of the Christian message there is momentum—an impetus to carry the life-changing experience of Christ into every part of the world (Matt. 28:19). The goal has been given, and all our strategy must somehow tend towards that one end. Every step towards its fulfilment is fuelled by heavenly power (Acts 1:8). We do this knowing that we are commanded (Mark 16:15), and on completion of this aim, we will precipitate the return of the King! (Matt. 24:14). The resulting new heaven and new earth will be populated by a great number drawn from every people group (Rev. 7:9, 10).

People groups

Although the truth of Jesus does not change, the way in which that truth is expressed does. There are approximately 6500 recognisably distinct languages in the world. None of us would suggest that we present the gospel in a tongue that our particular hearer could not understand. We need to present the gospel in such a way that any barrier of language or culture can be transcended, and our hearers can receive the truth in an accessible form.

To achieve this, we cannot be limited in our view of nations as defined by territorial boundaries between countries. The Greek word *ethnos* is used in most of the above verses, and can be translated as 'nations'. Originally it was a word applied to a multitude, and later to a nation or people. Similarly *laos* in Revelation speaks of 'a people' sharing a characteristic such as race or language. There are many nations which do not have the geographical and political status of a country, for instance, Armenians, Tamils and Gypsies. Distinct groups can be found within these larger communities, based on common ties of history, geography and beliefs. It is easy to see that each country is composed of tens or even hundreds of 'nations'. These homogeneous groups of people are thought of as people groups.

Donald McGavran has spoken of 'the magnificent and intricate mosaic of mankind represented by the world's cultures'. He goes on to say, 'The adaptation of Christianity to the cultures of each piece of the mosaic is crucially important.'[1]

Culture shifts

The cultural background of a people makes a significant difference to the choices that individuals are likely to make. It does not determine them; it simply makes some easier than others. We have seen dramatic changes take place in Eastern Europe, and have observed how the prevailing framework of society has influenced people's responses. For this reason, we need to know how the world is changing on a global level. This background will influence any evangelistic strategy that we may develop.

a) Globalisation

The interests, thinking and behaviour of people across the world now have more in common, thanks to advances in global transport, and in world-wide media. A marketing idea on one side of the world can result in purchases in a very different society on the other. The expression of political desires in one group can stir up similar activities in a people who are far distant both geographically and culturally.

---

1. Quoted in Howard A. Snyder, *The Problem of Wineskins* (Intervarsity Press of America, 1975) page 152.

b) Migration
We are seeing massive shifts, sometimes of whole population groups within a country, across a region or even throughout the world.

c) Nationalism
Perhaps in part because of the effect of globalisation, more and more ethnic groups are striving to maintain their identity in a distinct cultural, linguistic and increasingly political way. The break-up of the old Soviet dominions and Yugoslavia has given us graphic evidence of the determination of people to assert what they see as their corporate identity.

d) Urbanisation
By the end of the century, there will be 300 world-class cities, each with more than 1 million inhabitants. There is a continued shift of people away from rural areas into cities, where the large number of poor looking for money and work often creates an 'underclass' on the margins of society. It is projected that as many as 80% of the world's population will be in cities by the year 2000. This compares with only 15% at the start of the century.

e) Utilitarianism
Increasingly, a more materialistic view of the world is having its effect. People and things are seen only in terms of their functional usefulness. This means that concepts and individuals are not always seen as having value in their own right and become exploitable and expendable.

f) Consumerism
Vast efforts are made to make sure that markets are global. Often the driving force behind political decisions and social experience is the wealth to be made in satisfying the real or perceived needs of the consumer.

g) Secularisation
Religious thought and practice are seen as having little to offer the everyday running of a twentieth-century

state. There is a separation of what is seen as mainstream activity in society and religious thought and practice. It is increasingly viewed as an optional leisure activity. This can be true even within Islamic societies. To quote Salman Rushdie from an article in the *Guardian* ('Islamic Curses', 13 July 1994), 'Secularism demands a total separation between church and state in the Muslim world.'

h) Nominalism

This results in an increasing tendency for people to feel some sort of traditional or cultural allegiance to a religion, but to be personally detached and uncommitted to its daily practice and underlying philosophy. For instance, Christianity is a powerful influence in Norway, where before the recent elections the party leaders were debating theological differences on the Second Coming! However, although 97% of the population consider themselves affiliated to the church, only 5% actually attend!

i) Pluralism

There is a very strong trend towards ignoring the exclusive claims of any set of beliefs and instead encouraging an acceptance of all on equal merit. This is based on the belief that all value and truth is relative, and that there are no absolutes. Convenience takes the place of commitment, and in politics decisions are made according to what is expedient rather than what may be right.

Reasons for hope

With the end of the Cold War, there has been a realignment of the world order. We are seeing the emergence of regional power blocs which seem much more transient and unpredictable than the previous superpower stand-off. In this new and dangerous world, we should take the opportunity to overcome barriers to the gospel as we find them. Indeed, worldwide the church has been doing this successfully, and there is much to thank God for.

We are living in a world where for the first time in human history we see a global outpouring of the Holy Spirit. Four-fifths of the world is experiencing unprecedented growth in the church, marked by miracles and revival. This is by no means touching every area and people group represented within those areas, but there is certainly a quantum leap in the spread of the gospel.

Consider the following :

- The world population is growing by 1.7% each year. The church is increasing by 3% and charismatic evangelicals by 8%.
- Each day, there are 78,000 new Christians.
- Each week there are 1600 new churches.
- Over 3% of the world's population are charismatic/Pentecostal.
- Three-quarters of the world's ethnic groups have a viable church.

During this century, it is estimated that the number of evangelical Christians worldwide will have grown from 50 million to 2000 million! In Latin America, that change has been from 50 thousand to 137 million. In Africa, from 10 million to 324 million! No wonder that African evangelists are aiming to present the entire continent as a gift to God to mark the millennium! (This includes the Muslim North!)

In this final decade it is estimated that 4.3 million churches will be planted. In the year 2000, 70 million Bibles will be sold, 25 thousand new Christian books will be published, and 1 billion will hear the gospel by radio! In an age which likes to play down success, and a church that often plans for decline rather than growth, it is good to know that God is at work and on target to fulfil the work of global evangelisation!

The unreached

Before the euphoria lulls us into false complacency, we need to know that although the achievements are spectacular, there is still much to be done. In the year 2000, there will be 6.5 billion people. At present there are about 12 thousand ethno-linguistic people groups that are totally unreached, that is, they have no presentation of the gospel. Most of these are in the largely unevangelised section of the world known as 'the 10/40 window'. This is Africa, the Middle East and Asia between 10 and 40 degrees of latitude north of the equator.

To reach these people and hasten the return of the King, the church has to understand their particular linguistic and cultural problems and the changing trends outlined above.

It is good that by the end of the decade, two-thirds of the world's Christians will be outside the cultural West. It is also excellent that in the eighties there was a threefold increase in the number of missionaries sent out of the 'Two-Thirds World', so that they now total about 30% of the global number. Within this broader base of backgrounds, it will be much easier to promote accessible evangelism for the groups so far unrepresented in the Kingdom.

Dawn 2000

This project seeks to mobilise the church in every nation into fulfilling the goal of world evangelisation. Its aim is to see a congregation in existence in every small group of every kind, class and condition of people in each country. The strategy is explained in Jim Montgomery's book of the same name.[2] By 1995, it is hoped that every country on earth will have the beginning of a DAWN project. If this is to be achieved, it is estimated that on top of the 3 million churches that exist now, there will be

2. Montgomery, Jim, *Dawn 2000: 7 million churches to go* (William Carey Library, 1989)

7 million more churches planted by the end of this decade. This will mean that there is then a congregation for every 600 people.

It may seem a difficult target to attain, but to quote McGavran again, the goal is 'to multiply in every piece of the magnificent mosaic, truly Christian churches which fit that piece, are closely adapted to its culture, and recognised by its non-Christians as 'our kind of show'.[3]

3. McGavran, quoted in Snyder, op. cit.

CHAPTER 3

CROSSING CULTURES IN THE OLD TESTAMENT

Religious culture and national identity are inseparable in the Old Testament. Because of God's identification with Israel as His special people, we would not necessarily expect to find much in this part of the Bible about crossing cultures. However, there is in fact a very strong unfolding revelation towards this end. It starts with the relationship with God of one man, Abraham, and directly points towards the fulfilment of God's desire for relationship with every people group.

Setting the scene

In Genesis 4, we see a multiplication of sin and violence with successive generations. Through the flood, God permitted a fresh start, and entered into a covenant with Noah which affected the whole earth (Gen. 9:8–17).

Although the nations then spread out across the earth, they are described as a large homogeneous group with easy communication and spread of influence (Gen. 10:32; 11:1). It seems that pride led to rebellion, and the kingdom of humanity threatened to exclude any rule of God. This was graphically highlighted at the Tower of Babel. Into this situation came confusion, and lack of co-operation. From it came the separation into independent people groups marked by different languages (Gen. 11:1–9). Later, the call of God came to Abraham, asking him to leave behind all the symbols and values of his upbringing. His was to be a literal and spiritual journey of faith (Gen. 12:1–5).

At the very origin of the people of Israel was a call to a different culture.

Israel as a distinctive group

The emerging nation acknowledged a faith in one God, making them very different from their neighbours. This special relationship with God was crystallised in a unique national covenant and marked physically in circumcision (Gen. 17:1–16). In time, their identity was expressed geographically by the possession of the Promised Land (Exod. 23:31). Even in the outworking of the covenant which made Israel so distinct was God's desire to impact the wider world. In Exodus 34:10: 'The people you live among will see how awesome is the work that I, the Lord, will do for you.'

Israel was to be an earthly representation of God's kingdom, a community in whom spiritual holiness was symbolised by physical cleansing and perfection. Every part of personal and community life was touched by the values and symbols of their beliefs. God had identified with Israel as His chosen people (Deut. 7:6). Their cultural integrity was supported by dietary laws, codes of personal and public conduct, and religious symbols reminding them of God's presence such as the tablets and the Ark. Israel came together as a community of the redeemed in religious acts such as the sin offerings and the Atonement (Lev. 4:14; 16:21).

The book of Numbers describes Israel as a set of families and tribes who together make up a nation amongst whom God pitches His tent. Their shared knowledge was to be passed on within the families (Deut. 4:9). They were encouraged to keep themselves separate from other people groups and not to intermarry (1 Kgs. 11:2).

Despite their strong sense of national identity, the

nation was reminded that they were aliens in God's lands (Lev. 25:23). Undoubtedly it was a major feature in their survival during times of hardship and persecution. In Egypt, the nation experienced attempts at 'ethnic cleansing' and demands to increase productivity whilst cutting resources (Exod 1:22; 5:7). They retained their culture in the face of exile (Ps. 137), and endured slander, manipulation and rejection at different stages (Ezra 4:15; Neh. 4:1, 2). Efforts were made to enforce the worship of alternative deities (Dan. 3:12). They miraculously escaped from the hatred which erupted in Haman's edict—the final attempt to destroy the Jewish nation recorded in the Old Testament (Esther 3:6).

Foreigners in the Old Testament

At a time when God spoke largely to and through Israel, it is interesting to see how revelation broke through from people of a different cultural heritage. In this way, He showed that relationship with Him involved faith, obedience and guidance, not just racial origin and cultural correctness. Even at the times of Israel's greatness, God was pointing the way to His purpose of involving all nations, not just one.

There are some wonderful examples of how non-Israelites were used to the benefit of the chosen people. As has been mentioned before, Abraham, the great father and hero of the nation, started as an outsider. One of the most fascinating characters of the Old Testament was Melchizedek from Salem. He was the original prophet, priest and king who blessed Abraham (Gen. 14:18–20). He was spoken of as a prefigure of Christ (Heb. 7:1–17), and yet did not share any of the same national origin.

Balaam was also greatly used to bless and prophesy over the people of Israel, although with some reluctance. He could even foresee the coming of Jesus (Num. 22; 24:17). Rahab the prostitute from Jericho was an example of faith (Josh. 6:25), and Cyrus the king of Persia perceived the hand of God at work in the world (Ezra 1:2).

One of the most moving stories must surely be that of Ruth the Moabitess. Because of her faith and loyalty she wanted to identify with Naomi's people Israel. As a result, she gained a place in David's ancestry, and so subsequently in the genealogy of Jesus. This is certainly a demonstration of how all nations will have a part in the Kingdom of God's greater Son (Ruth 1:17; 2:10).

In 2 Kings chapter 5, we read of Naaman the commander of the Aramean army. He suffers from leprosy, and having heard of Elisha through a servant girl, goes to find healing. He reacts against the prescription of bathing in the river Jordan with predictable national pride, but overcomes his prejudice, and is healed. This shows the power of God not being restricted to Israel alone, and Naaman even raises the difficult question of how far he may compromise his new belief with the cultural expectations demanded of him once he goes home. Naaman asks to take home some soil from Israel on which to worship God. There is a revelation of the reality of the presence of God outside Israel's geographical boundaries, although the soil is a symbol of that presence.

The existence of the Temple was an inspiration to cultural identity in Israel, but even this important symbol included outsiders. A man of mixed parentage was put in charge of crafting all the bronze furnishings (1 Kgs. 7:13). Foreigners were told that their prayers would be answered if they prayed towards it (1 Kgs. 8:41–43). In the original Temple of Solomon, room had not yet been created for the Gentiles, but in Herod's construction a court was built especially to accommodate foreign proselytes. Perhaps this was the result of increasing understanding of God's wider purpose.

Within the law and practice of Israel, provision was made for those of a different ethnic origin, the 'aliens'. Outsiders were not to be ill-treated (Exod. 22:21; Lev. 19:33, 34). Fairness and love were to be shown towards them (Deut. 1:16; 10:19). Foreigners were even to be included in the major religious rituals that marked Israel's status (Lev. 17:8; 24:16; Deut. 16:14; Josh. 8:35). Although this was not always adhered to, there are passages of the nation's history which demonstrate such devotion such as the sparing of the Egyptian (1 Sam. 30:13) and the avenging of the Gibeonites (2 Sam. 21). Ebedmelech the Cushite, who showed such kindness to Jeremiah, was spared during the destruction of Jerusalem 'because you trust in me, declares the Lord' (Jer. 39:18).

The book of Jonah is all about the exploits of the reluctant prophet being sent to speak the need for repentance to the non-Jewish people of Nineveh. He knows that God will not be able to resist sparing the people, even though in Jonah's view they deserve the destruction he is sent to warn them about.

In the Old Testament, there is a growing realisation and demonstration that God's care and provision are not limited by territory and race. We see a gradual development of the ideal that truth and salvation should be for the Gentiles also, and that the whole world should be God's domain.

Other groups

Attention was given to people who found themselves in situations which could be vulnerable. There was some measure of understanding towards those who needed the protection of Israel's close tribal system. They were to be included in the provision, both spiritual and material, that Israel enjoyed. These were typified by the grouping together of 'the widow, the orphan, and the alien' in the law. We have already referred to the alien, but the group as a whole was used as a shorthand to mean any who did not quite fit into the tight cultural framework because of origin or family circumstances. The nation was encouraged to take up this responsibility in order to access these subgroups of their society.

- Their rights were to be defended (Deut. 10:18)
- They were included in religious ritual (Deut. 16:11)
- Provision was made for them at harvest (Deut. 24:21)
- Tithing was to be set aside for their use (Deut. 26:12)

In a nation that could easily become male-orientated, we see the position of women established in a variety of ways. Deborah was called to lead Israel (Judg. 4:4). Those without visible support were given aid, such as the widow at Zarephath and the widow of one of the prophets (1 Kgs. 17:9; 2 Kgs. 4:1). The inheritance of Zelophehad's daughters was protected (Num. 27:7).

The poor were not to be ignored (Ps. 82:3), and the old should not be marginalised (Ps. 71:9). The story of David's restoration of the crippled Mephibosheth is an inspiration in the inclusion of the disabled (2 Sam. 9:1–13). Even those of doubtful sexuality, the eunuchs, could be identified as being on the side of the men of God (2 Kgs. 9:32).

Towards all peoples

It was always God's intention that the chosen people would demonstrate His rule and nature to the world. As the occupation of the Promised Land proceeds in the book of Joshua, no booty is taken, as a sign that land already belongs to God and is not simply the result of human conquest. Israel was to be marked out as a witness and blessing to the nations of the earth. Ultimately this would involve the coming of Jesus first as the sacrifice for all, and again as the ruler of all.

Amongst the nations of the world Israel was to do the following:

- make a name for God (2 Sam. 7:23)
- prove His uniqueness (2 Kgs. 19:19)

- proclaim what He had done (Ps. 9:11)
- bring praise and sing of God (Ps. 57:9)
- be a light to the Gentiles (Isa. 49:6)
- create a house of prayer for all (Isa. 56:7)
- provide prophets (Jer. 1:5).

In the Old Testament there is an expanding revelation of God's desire to make His truth accessible to all nations and people groups. Even the apparently *exclusive* nature of Israel's religious culture was to lead into a demonstration of the *inclusive* nature of God's heart. A new relationship based on heart change and the Holy Spirit is offered, which transcends the national covenant (Ezek. 36:26, 27).

A spiritual awareness is developed into which the Messiah can come, bringing salvation not only to the Jews but to everyone. He is described as the 'banner for the nations' (Isa. 5:26), and the 'desired' of all nations (Hag. 2:7). He will establish a reign of justice for all (Isa. 42:1), and will be worshipped by 'all peoples, nations and men of every language' (Dan. 7:14). As a result of the coming of Jesus, it is promised that 'all the ends of the earth will see the salvation of our God' (Isa. 52:10).

Finally we can look forward to the day when all nations will be God's people (Zech. 2:11), when representatives of every people group will be priests (Isa. 66:21), and in every place there will be pure worship (Mal. 1:11).

CHAPTER 4

JESUS—THE CROSS-CULTURAL LIFE

The four gospels are intended to communicate the life of Jesus to a wide audience. Matthew is written as a testimony to Jewish people, and so draws on experiences with which they would be familiar. The writer continually refers back to the Old Testament and shows how Jesus links in to prophecy and tradition. It assumes a background different to that of the audience for which Luke writes. He is clearly communicating with Gentiles, including the named Theophilus. He does not attempt to include much from Jewish tradition, but instead gives careful accounts, typical of a trained physician, from an eyewitness perspective. Interestingly, he makes a lot of the place of women, and of the information he clearly gleaned from women, including Mary (Luke 2:19).

The life of Jesus

The early life of Jesus involved a cultural mix. His birth was attended by shepherds, the representatives of a lowly class. As a toddler, He was visited by wealthy Gentiles, the wise men. He and His parents escaped to Egypt as refugees. When He was presented at the Temple, the elderly Simeon prophesied that the baby in arms would be 'a light for revelation to the Gentiles and for glory to your people Israel' (Luke 2:32). This dual theme of inclusion for both Jews and non-Jews picked up from the Old Testament is strongly expanded throughout the New.

Jesus grew up in Nazareth in the region of Galilee. There were cultural differences between Galileans and the more sophisticated southerners from around Jerusalem. This is hinted at by Matthew when he quotes Isaiah referring to the Messiah coming from 'Galilee of the Gentiles' (Matt. 4:15). He also mentions 'the way to the sea'. This was a caravan route from Egypt to Damascus which passed just behind Nazareth. Jesus did not grow up in an isolated backwater. Close to His home town lay the junction of three caravan routes and a Roman road. As a boy Jesus would have been familiar with Syrian, Phoenician, Arab and Roman travellers.

Jesus and people

Although those that Jesus invited to be His disciples were all Jewish, they came from a variety of subcultures. There were fishermen, including one who was familiar in the circles of the high priest (John 18:15, 16). Nathanael was devout and Thomas was a sceptic. Matthew the tax collector rubbed shoulders with Simon the Zealot. Judas Iscariot was the only southerner in a company of Galileans. Philip was unafraid to introduce Greeks to Jesus (John 12:20, 21). In His extended team were a group of women who also represented several social groups (Luke 8:2, 3).

Jesus crossed many cultural boundaries, in mixing with people, that respectable religious Jews did not cross. He spent time with tax collectors (Matt. 21:32) and royal officials (John 4:46) as well as the ruler of a synagogue (Mark 5:22). Respected rabbis and children were His companions (John 3:10; Mark 9:36). Jesus esteemed the poor widow (Luke 21:2), reprieved an adulteress (Luke 7:44–50), and invited a criminal to Paradise (Luke 23:40–43). He was prepared to respond to the needs of people with various sicknesses (Matt. 4:24), and to be touched by a ritually unclean woman (Matt. 9:20). He was not afraid to mix with the violent and demonised (Matt. 8:28), have contact with lepers

(Luke 17:11–19), or with the dead (Mark 5:21–43). All of these were culturally unacceptable.

Jewish people tried to avoid involvement with foreigners, and thought of them as less than human. Jesus provided all outsiders with an unsurpassed dignity. Roman centurions received a good report from Jesus, who used one as a model to understand kingdom authority (Matt. 8:5–13). He provoked fury by implying that the Canaanite woman had faith of a type unknown in Israel (Matt. 15:21–28). Simon of Cyrene was given the honour of carrying the Messiah's cross. He was clearly not Jewish as the Roman soldiers would not have risked a riot by pressing a Jew into unclean service on the eve of Passover (Matt. 27:32).

The main targets of popular prejudice in Israel were the Samaritans. They were the descendants of the survivors of the northern kingdom after the fall of Samaria in 722 BC. They had intermarried with foreigners who were forcibly moved into the area. As their culture diverged from Jerusalem and the southern kingdom, they built their own temple on Mount Gerizim. This was destroyed by a Jewish king. The historical and racial separation grew with time into outright enmity. Into this division Jesus brought reconciliation. He was ready to enter a Samaritan village (Luke 9:52), and healed men who were not only lepers but Samaritan lepers (Luke 17:16). He broke many social mores by speaking with the woman at the well (John 4), and in effect identified with a model of his own response in the description of the Samaritan in the well-known parable, the Good Samaritan (Luke 10:25–37).

The teaching of Jesus

Jesus was always concerned that His message should reach those for whom it was intended. He recognised that not everyone would be open and ready to receive it at the same time. This would be due more to their spiritual state than to any difficulty in communication. Jesus used stories, picture language and everyday items in His desire to put across truth. This He was able to do so skilfully that the message could be interpreted simultaneously on several different levels, all of them valid, depending on the character and experience of the hearer. In the same sermon He could motivate the uneducated and challenge the intellect of the Pharisees.

Jesus took concepts that were familiar to all, and situations that He could actually point to as object lessons while speaking. For instance, when Jesus was teaching outside, as He so often did, He made ample use of the obvious, such as the vineyard, fields, sheep and goats, and the sower. In a pastoral environment everyone knew these well. Familiar objects could speak of eternal truth when in the hands of Jesus. Bread, wine, water, seed, lamps—all took on a new meaning. He deliberately took the visual and used it to convey a greater unseen reality.

Jesus used ideas and symbols that were culturally appropriate. He spoke to a fisherman about 'fishing for men', to a centurion about authority, and to religious people about sacred tradition. He took what people knew to be true in their experience and invested it with a fresh level of insight. The way in which Jesus communicated His truth was always relevant to those who heard.

Some of the settings that Jesus used were crucial. For example, He chose the road just outside Caesarea Philippi to ask the disciples, 'Who do you say I am?' (Mark 8:27–29). This was not an idle question to pass away the journey. This city was the centre of the Roman occupation of the region. Set into the hillside on the main road leading into the city were many shrines. This enabled soldiers from all over the Roman Empire to pay homage to their favourite deity. Surrounded by the effigies of a hundred false gods, Jesus provokes His friends into stating His divine identity!

The Son of God was prepared to challenge and stimulate in order to gain a response. He was willing to come up against the preconceptions inherent in the prevailing cultural traditions in order to present a greater truth. Jesus told the Pharisees 'You have let go of the commands of God and are holding on to the traditions of men' (Mark 7:8). He hit at the heart of religion to replace it with reality. He reassessed the value of the Sabbath according to people's needs (Luke 13:10–17). Jesus threw out the moneychangers (Matt. 21:12), and compared favourably the repentant tax collector with the religious bigot (Luke 18:9–14). Jesus challenged the accepted values of materialism, family life, leadership and power. John 13 relates His demonstration of servanthood, proving His eloquence through actions as well as words. His refusal to conform crossed cultural territory in the minds of His followers.

The ultimate adventure

Jesus was quite clear that His message would involve representatives of all nations. When He announced the manifesto of the Kingdom in the synagogue at Nazareth, His religious hearers were unable to accept either Jesus or His teaching. As He identified Himself with the fulfilment of Messianic prophecy, He spoke of liberation for some of the most rejected and marginalised in Jewish society (Luke 4:18–19).

When the townsfolk rejected His identity, Jesus pointed them to the Old Testament to show that as Jews rejected God's fulfilment of redemption, the Messiah would be sent to the non-Jews (Luke 4:24–27). He is recorded as saying that He came as a light for all people (John 1:9) and to be the light for the whole world (John 8:12). Indeed Jesus spoke of having sheep belonging to flocks other than those of the Jews (John 10:16), and that people from the east and the west would sit at the heavenly banquet with the Jewish patriarchs (Matt. 8:11). This controversial teaching overthrowing the cultural prejudices of His fellow Jews would not have made for popular preaching!

As he prepared to see Jesus put to death, Caiaphas prophesied that He would die for the Jewish nation, but John comments 'not only for that nation, but also for the scattered children of God' (John 11:51, 52). At the time of the ultimate sacrifice which paid the price for global salvation, Pilate unwittingly made a prophetic statement. He had a notice nailed to the cross proclaiming 'Jesus of Nazareth, the King of the Jews' (John 19:19–20), and this statement was written for non-Jews in Aramaic, Latin and Greek—the commonly spoken language of the Roman world.

The heart of Jesus was broken for all upon the cross. It did not matter whether they were Jewish or Gentile, or from whatever time, location, race or subgroup. All He looks for is a response to His loving invitation based on faith. No other criteria is necessary. With the knowledge of this universal opportunity, it is no wonder that He tells us to 'Go!' We go to every people group in obedience to His command (Matt. 28:19, 20), knowing that one day when the reality of Jesus is culturally accessible to all, Father will call time and the Son will return! (Matt. 24:14)

CHAPTER 5

CROSSING CULTURES IN THE NEW TESTAMENT

In the book of Acts, Luke documents the outward explosion of belief from Jerusalem. The church changes from being a Jewish sect, 'The Way', into a movement capable of incorporating all national groupings. The action shifts both actually and symbolically from Jerusalem to Antioch and beyond.

Jesus gave the nucleus of the early church the directive: 'You will be my witnesses in Jerusalem, and in all Judea and Samaria, and to the ends of the earth' (Acts 1:8). So what did they do? Stay in Jerusalem! It seems that they still could not perceive the universal appeal of Christ outside a Jewish context.

Development of mission

The first shift in thinking is seen in Acts chapter 2, when the Holy Spirit fills the disciples, and they go out into the street speaking in tongues. These are recognisable by God-fearing Jews 'from every nation under heaven' (Acts 2:5). It is a supernatural reversal of the effect of the Tower of Babel. The fact that these men hear the apostles 'declaring the wonders of God in our own tongues!' is a major development in making truth accessible in the language of each hearer. Those who heard, though, were exclusively Jewish in religion and culture, and mainly by race, although a few would have been proselytes (Acts 2:11).

The church continues to expand rapidly in Jerusalem, but little is done to fulfil the strategy given by Jesus. That is, until God permits the winds of persecution following Stephen's martyrdom to scatter the church throughout Judea and Samaria. Even so, 'all except the apostles' left the religious centre Jerusalem! (Acts 8:1)

It was one of the deacons, Philip, who started an evangelistic mission to Samaria. Despite mass conversions, healings and deliverances, Philip had the humility to leave the action and find himself on a desert road in Gaza. The next significant step was about to take place. Here he meets a man who is a Jewish proselyte—a foreigner who has adopted the Jewish religion, but whose origins are from another continent and culture. As a result of Philip's explanation of the scriptures, this Ethiopian court official is saved. Although within fifty miles of Jerusalem, he is the first clearly identified Gentile believer. Tradition states that he returned to his home land and began what they claim to be the oldest Christian church in the world.

In chapter 10 of Acts, we read of the fundamental change in Peter's thinking as a result of the vision he was given regarding what can be classed as clean and unclean. A devout Roman, Cornelius, invited Peter to preach to a house full of Gentiles, contravening so many prejudices and taboos of Jewish practice. They are all saved! (Acts 10:34—11:18). This quantum shift in cultural approach required a direct revelation to the leader of the church in Jerusalem, and set the scene for the development of the worldwide church that was to follow.

This gave the momentum, and the permission, for others to go outside the territorial boundaries of Israel altogether. Some Greek-speaking Jews caught the vision, set off for Antioch, 'and began to speak to Greeks also' (Acts 11:20). In so doing, they laid the foundations of the pioneer missionary centre of the early church.

The Antioch principle

In chapter 13 of Acts, we witness the birth of missionary history. The impetus to cross cultural barriers is released. Within the leadership of the church were five people, each of whom were representative of vastly different backgrounds:

Barnabas—a Greek-speaking Jew from Cyprus
Simeon—called Niger (was he a black African?)
Manaen—the princely foster brother of Herod Antipas
Lucius—from North Africa
Saul/Paul—the orthodox highly trained rabbi

Few would have given such a varied leadership much chance of survival!

For me, the Antioch principle is this—if we wish to see the church at the heart of the world, then the world needs to be at the heart of the church. In other words, the desire to influence and to change the world is facilitated by a leadership that is representative of more than one group, and is able to express the needs of a broad spectrum of people.

It should come as no surprise to find that the Holy Spirit could breeze into their worship and fasting in order to set aside two-thirds of the core team. The church at Antioch prepared to part with their best for the sake of crossing cultures with the gospel. Ananias had already pointed the way forward for Paul. He had prophesied 'this man is my chosen instrument to carry my name before the Gentiles . . . and the people of Israel' (Acts 9:15). I wonder whether Ananias had ever asked himself the significance of God putting 'the Gentiles' first?

From Antioch, the great missionary adventure began. Paul and Barnabas set out for Pisidian Antioch, where it is recorded that they reached both the Jews and the Gentiles (Acts 13:16–46).

Place and people

The phrase 'Jews and Greeks' keeps on appearing throughout the New Testament as a kind of shorthand, meaning all people irrespective of their cultural origin. To the Jews, there were only two types of people in the world, those who were Jewish and those who were not!

It took a little time before the early church could break through racial and religious barriers. However, from the earliest days, the Holy Spirit enabled them to ignore social restrictions with the word, and with wonders. This is seen in the wide spectrum of people who had encounters with God in Acts—beggars, the chief priests and elders, widows, priests who joined the disciples, occult practitioners, soldiers, Roman officials, members of historic religions, prisoners, business people, students, children, sailors, a governor, and even members of the royal family!

On reading Luke's report, it is clear that Paul was ready to speak about Jesus at any opportunity. He deliberately chose places where people gathered, as well as where circumstance took him, and often places that were high profile. Amongst these were houses, market places, synagogues, a lecture hall, the roadside, prisons, the courtroom, a barracks, the riverside, on board ship, the seashore—taking the message to where people were rather than forcing them to come and find him in a special 'religious' building.

There are also very good examples of how Paul and others packaged the same truth in culturally acceptable forms, depending on their hearers. Stephen's remarkable speech as he faced death is recorded in Acts chapter 7. In it, he documents the religious history of the nation familiar to his listeners, but leading inexorably to the death of Jesus and the need for repentance. Although the main points he makes are unpalatable to his audience, Stephen builds from what they already know to be true.

In Lystra, Paul takes the misguided adoration of idol worshippers, and turns their attention from their created 'gods' to the Creator God. He starts from the understanding that he is offered rather than sticking to a fixed agenda of his own (Acts14:11–18). In Athens, he has the opportunity to preach amongst the social and educated elite at the Areopagus (Acts 17:16–31). He uses a totally different approach, appealing to the Athenians' inherent agnosticism, and quoting their own poets. In Corinth, Paul holds public discussions, and in Ephesus is forcefully direct. When he appears in court before King Agrippa, the apostle is courteous but definite. He brings elements into his preaching designed to appeal to the king's education, to his position, and to knowledge of Jewish custom (Acts 26).

Problems

It is often assumed that members of the early church were somehow more spiritual than we are. It is reassuring to find that they also faced difficult issues and struggled with the practical outworking of their theology! One of the problems was the complaint that the Hellenic Jews were being discriminated against in the daily food distribution. This distribution took place amongst those for whom the early church felt they had a responsibility. It would seem that the prejudice was real as well as perceived. The apostles solved the issues by devolving some measure of authority to an expanded level of leadership (Acts 6:1–6). This suggests that the early Christians were experiencing tensions of culture clash and prejudice.

This resurfaced later, when Jewish believers travelled to Antioch insisting that salvation was dependent upon the adoption of Jewish custom. Paul and Barnabas were despatched to Jerusalem to settle the situation. There was clearly a sharp discussion from opposing points of view. Peter had to remind the church leaders of the revelation that God had given him about the gospel not being bound by Jewish tradition. Barnabas and Paul were able to explain how God had been moving amongst the non-Jews. James, the leader of the Jerusalem church, took their attention back to the Old Testament, to justify theologically the argument they were putting forward. He then suggested a compromise solution. He advised that Gentiles observe four stipulations where they might have particular weaknesses, the violation of which would cause distress to their Jewish brothers. This was not to reinforce a prejudice, but was a practical solution making the contact between the two groups easier. This was then formulated into a letter, and circulated around the churches (Acts 15:1–29).

This did not put the matter to rest. Some time later, Paul was advised to make a public display of Jewish ritual by identifying himself with purification rites at the temple. This was in order to settle rumours that were being spread about his ministry, and that threatened to divide the early church (Acts 21:17–26).

The apostle to the Gentiles

Paul was prepared to take the truth about his God to whoever would listen. He saw the primacy of his own tradition, 'first for the Jew, then for the Gentile' (Rom. 2:10), but believed passionately that he was 'to call people from among all the Gentiles to the obedience that comes from faith' (Rom. 1:5). He wanted to appeal to all, to 'Greeks and non-Greeks' (Rom. 1:14). In order to do this there were times when he made much of his rabbinical heritage, and others when it was convenient to speak of being a Roman citizen (Acts 22:3, 25). Paul had impeccable Jewish credentials which he was not afraid to use (Phil. 3:4–5), but he also knew that above all else he could claim the description 'apostle to the Gentiles' (Rom. 11:13). He would not allow anything that he was, or that he said and did, to become an obstacle between another person and God. On the contrary, his intention was that these things should facilitate his evangelism. 'I have become all things to all men so that by all possible means I might save some' (1 Cor. 9:22).

Paul's commitment to all people groups was profound. He believed that it was possible for God to appeal to the consciences of non-Jewish people (Rom. 2:15), a radical teaching for the first century! He spoke of God being 'the father of all who believe' (Rom. 4:11), who looked for faith rather than religion. He described true Jewishness as being 'of the heart, by the spirit' rather than centred on outward observances such as circumcision (Rom. 2:29), and he included non-Jewish believers as 'children of the promise' (Rom. 9:8). Paul's Lord was 'of the Gentiles too' (Rom. 3:29), who did not treat people as outsiders, 'aliens', because of their different origin (Eph. 2:19). He believed racial and social backgrounds made no difference to God (Rom. 10:12), and so could proclaim, in an age governed by such differences, 'Here there is no Greek or Jew, circumcised or uncircumcised, barbarian, Scythian, slave or free, but Christ is all, and is in all' (Col. 3:11).

As we have seen, this revolutionary revelation was not easily or universally accepted within the first group of Christians. There were those who could not break out of the Jewish mindset, and wanted to keep the church as a Jewish sect. Paul told people to beware of the 'mutilators of the flesh' referring to their insistence on circumcision (Phil. 3:2). The whole of the letter to the Galatians is an appeal urging them not to go back under the bondage of tradition and law, to stop them from interpreting the gospel in a single cultural perspective. In it he refers to Peter and others, whom he had to oppose because of their hypocrisy in dealing with Jews and Gentiles (Gal. 2:3).

The apostle's openness was to those of differing social conditions also. The sublime letter he wrote to Philemon is the winning invitation for a wealthy friend to welcome back his fellow Christian, the runaway slave Onesimus. He uplifted the dignity of those who were not wise (1 Cor. 1:26), and those who could be considered weak (Rom. 14:14). His view of church was inclusive of people who were hungry (1 Cor. 4:11), and poor (2 Cor. 8:9). He commented on singleness and marriage, spoke about the family, and included the extremes of age (Eph. 5:22; 1 Tim. 5:2–5). He upgraded the place of women in his society.[1] Whilst in prison himself, Paul was able to share the truth of God with, on the one hand, fellow prisoners, and on the other, members of his captor's household! (Phil. 1:12, 4:22). In reality he could proclaim, 'We were all baptised by one spirit into one body—whether Jews or Greeks, slave or free' (1 Cor. 12:13).

Other streams

Paul was not the only leader within the early church to make culture an important issue. Other successful attempts were made to cross cultural barriers and to make truth accessible. The writer of the letter to the Hebrews, in my view Barnabas, composed an outstanding sonnet to the glory of Jesus. The descriptions, allusions and imagery were all based in the traditions and ritual of Jewish belief and practice. He was making his message relevant and understandable to a particular readership.

James encourages the early church not to be so impressed by the symbols and power of wealth that they show favouritism (Jas. 2:1–7). He expects the church to assimilate people from different classes of society. Peter values the presence of both the old and the young in the fellowship (1 Pet. 5:1–5). He also reinterprets the traditional view of nationhood for the Jews to include all: 'But you are a chosen people, a royal priesthood, a holy nation' (1 Pet. 2:9).

The future

In Revelation, John gives us an exciting prospect in the

---

1. There are two excellent books in this series which look at the issues of singleness and the place of women in depth: *Better Than or Equal To?* by Linda Harding, and *The Role and Ministry of Women* by Martin Scott.

new heaven and the new earth. He saw 'a great multitude that no-one could count, from every nation, tribe, people and language' who were in the presence of the Lamb (Rev. 7:9). He saw an angel proclaiming the gospel to every people group on earth (Rev. 14:6) so that 'all nations will come and worship before you' (Rev. 15:4). We are told that Jesus will be the light to the nations, and that the tree of life will bring healing to them also (Rev. 21:24; 22:2). Every group, regardless of any distinctive or separating factor, will be represented there.

The final description of Jesus in the Bible is His identification with two prophetic titles (Rev. 22:16). The first is 'the Root and Offspring of David'. Although this is clearly from a Jewish context, Isaiah speaks the original in relation to the Gentiles also (Isa. 11:10). The second, 'the bright Morning Star' is something which can be seen by all people regardless of background, and was originally proclaimed by the non-Jewish prophet Balaam! (Num. 24:17). It is fitting that at the close of the New Testament we see Jesus as the fulfilment of both Jew and Gentile.

CHAPTER 6

CULTURE IN THE CHURCH

We cannot pretend that culture has no place in church. It will be there whether we like it or not. The issue is how far it will facilitate or obstruct the message that we communicate. There is a popular view of the traditional church that is often heard in conversation and portrayed in the media. That is of an institution which is largely irrelevant to the lives of the majority of people. I would tend to agree with this view.

The church in the UK has been in decline since 1916. The 1989 Church Census figures showed that in the previous decade, there had been a net loss from congregations of 1000 people every week. 70% of that loss had been in people under the age of twenty, with half in the late teenage years. In other words, when people were of an age to make up their own minds, they tended to vote with their feet. During that decade, the church was getting older and less relevant to an emerging generation which is increasingly unchurched. When interviewed, those leaving the church in this younger age band quoted boredom and lack of relevance as the main factors.

I once heard of a local doctor being visited by the minister of the church which was next door to his surgery. 'Why is it that we never see you in church on a Sunday?' the minister asked.

'Because half your congregation are in here on a Monday,' was the swift reply.

The outsider's view

Most people perceive a difference between what they believe the church is called to do, and what it actually does. There is a credibility gap for the traditional church at a time when many people are looking for reality. This may be seen in the popular expectation that senior clerics should believe in the foundations of the Christian faith, or that Christians should behave according to a morality which outsiders themselves would not keep. It is interesting that few people have a problem with Jesus—just the church.

It is very difficult to generalise, but there are certain recurring complaints raised against the church. Many people do not believe that the church is willing to tackle issues which are important to them, and think that it will answer tough questions with a call to faith alone, without reference to reason. There is an inclination to think that practical considerations are not taken into account, and that religious jargon replaces common sense. People are seen as projects, with an amiable shallowness taking the place of friendship. Christians seem dull, and sexually, if not emotionally, handicapped, while churches are exclusive and conservative. We as Christians may want to react strongly against such views as grossly misleading and unfair. However, people did not get this from encountering Jesus, but from what they have seen of the church. There exists a subculture marked out by behaviour patterns, language, symbols and a belief system which is not found elsewhere, and is therefore seen as irrelevant outside it.

The response of church to society

Many churches have put a theological gulf between themselves and the society of which they should still be a part. Non-Christians are seen as unholy and worldly, with society reflecting only the degenerate character of humankind. Any activity or movement within that society will be rejected as well. This may be true, for instance, with popular music. It is viewed as too 'worldly' to be used in church. Such a division between what is considered 'sacred' and 'secular' is unknown in the New Testament. It certainly cannot be seen in the life or teaching of Jesus. What happens then is that the prevailing culture within the church is acceptable, and anything else is not. The determining factors are not scriptural but cultural.

The interesting thing is that after ten or twenty years, what was previously 'unholy' becomes acceptable within the church, so the church ends up being permanently behind the times, catching up with what was happening outside decades before. To quote Gerald Coates, 'God will not be tied down to seventeenth-century language, eighteen-century songs, nineteenth-century morality and twentieth-century jargon.'

Practices are often decided according to taste and preference rather than the Bible, but these decisions can take on a theological status. After I had spoken in a denominational church about the reality of worship, one lady took me to task. She was upset that I had not included the organ on an overhead of biblical references. I tried to convince her that the instrument had not been invented for hundreds of years after the Bible had been completed, but it was in vain! Cultural patterns rather than principles are often the cause of division within a local church. Such patterns may be more important and provoke more loyalty than any scriptural truth they are meant to represent. Try asking the average attender in many churches why the fellowship practises its particular form of baptism and see what answers are given!

Church culture usually maintains the status quo. Culture may actually determine much of church life and structure. The church becomes culture bound. When threatened, people take refuge in culture. They may develop a 'siege mentality' and hold onto it even more strongly when facing change. This means that others are only likely to be welcomed if they fit into what already exists. The church becomes a homogeneous group by choice, and would have little chance of breaking out of this, even if the desire was there. Outsiders are asked to adapt to the prevailing culture inside the church, if they wish to become part of the fellowship.

Primary groups

Observers can describe groups of people who associate together for whatever purpose in particular ways. These dynamics can be true whether we seek to describe a club, an organisation or a church. Most churches in the UK can be described as 'primary groups'. There are certain characteristics which tend to be true of all primary groups. They tend to consist of 60 to 80 people who have a shared culture from the past. They have become an end in themselves and do not seek change. Primary groups are hard to grow and very strong. Individuals within these groups gain great security from their resistance to change. The purpose of primary groups is survival and control.

The whole momentum of the gospel involves change. Change as an individual, change in relationships, change in society: ultimately the change to a new heaven and a new earth. As Christians, we accept the need to change. We expect it, we encourage it, and we hope to cause it. The unwillingness or inability of churches to face necessary change is the root cause of their irrelevance. I do not mean 'change for change's sake'—that often-quoted phrase which is the kneejerk reaction of a threatened primary group—although frankly, almost any change can be beneficial compared with no change at all. I mean change which allows us and our message to be more accessible to people who need to hear it.

Church situations

Many of the features within church life started off for good reasons. Now, as times and people have changed, these features are no longer as appropriate as they once were.

a) Time

It is interesting to consider why church services start at particular times. In one area they told me it was to allow farmers who were milking to do their work and then attend the meetings. In another town it was due to the lighting times of gas lamps and when servants were allowed off on a Sunday. The problem is that these churches no longer consist of milking farmers and off-duty servants! I have also been told that the traditional late-morning service came from Luther's drinking habits, making it difficult for him to get out any earlier!

In some churches the possibility of not having a Sunday meeting would be unthinkable. As my Messianic Jewish friends have told me, Sunday never was the Sabbath. There is nothing special about this day over any other, although it may be more convenient for our meetings. Our expectations concerning how others keep time, or their use of calendars and diaries, may say a lot about our cultural and class background. There are those who speak of the use of filofaxes, while in their audience are many who do not possess a watch! On the other hand, consistently to arrive late may be reasonably construed as lack of commitment.

b) Worship

Jesus spoke of worship being 'in spirit and in truth'. In many churches the worship is of a bygone age in words and music, with little common ground for those who have not grown up in such a culture. They forget that the great hymns of Wesley and others were written to popular tunes of their day in order to convey scriptural theology. That style and vocabulary will not fulfil today the original intentions for which they were written.

Preferences in popular music styles are often determined within a few years of the teenage years, so our own likes and dislikes may result in a narrow band of style choice. We forget that what we think is modern becomes less so with each passing year. The commonplace soft rock style of worship music may appeal to the leaders, but not necessarily to others. We must also be careful that the average age of our worship band does not simply get older! It is also worth pointing out that complaints of the charismatic church against the 'five-hymn sandwich' can be matched by reservations about the mandatory repetitions of contemporary worship songs.

We may think that we experience freedom when the reality is something different. I remember sitting in a fellowship that I used to visit where they prided themselves on being free and 'open to the Holy Spirit'. I would sit looking at my watch, and could predict exactly who would stand up, when they would stand up, and what they would do when they did! This was not discernment on my part, but habit on theirs.

A Jewish teenager once compained to me that he had injured his back. He explained that the synagogue had been celebrating one of the festivals the previous weekend. He descibed how it was customary for all the young men to be involved in riotous dancing on these occasions, and that somehow he must have strained himself! I found myself wishing that we Christians could be so uninhibited in expressing praise with our bodies that we might risk physical injury!

It would be good to see a wider mix of cultural flavours represented in worship. Then people from other ethnic and social groups could see that we are not identifying Christ particularly with Western culture. There can be difficulties. We work extensively with Tamils, the majority of whom come from a Hindu background. They are happy to see drama in worship, but at first usually have problems over dance. This is because they are used to seeing dance intimately associated with the Hindu temple. It takes sensitivity and the Holy Spirit to overcome such a genuine cause of misunderstanding.

c) Vocabulary

We must never forget the sacrificial work done by the early pioneers who fought for the availability of the Bible in English. We must take great care not to cloud that accessibility by 'in-speak' which by its nature is only understood by the insider. Religious jargon may be useful as a shorthand to refer to a complex concept, but should be kept to a minimum. Sometimes the style of language we use, or the pitch of its educational level, is inappropriate for some. Traditionally, the lecture style is used for preaching, but in a society that is used to fast-moving media with an emphasis more on the visual than the spoken, the only time in people's lives that they are asked to sit and listen for any length of time may be in church.

d) Modelling

We give examples by *who we are* as well as *what we say.* What do visitors see when they come into many church meetings? Sometimes the use of a stage may imply performance rather than worship. A row of leaders facing the congregation may suggest superiority and exclusion. The appearance of only one person leading will speak of 'one-man ministry'. Sometimes people do not realise that there are women, children and ethnic groups involved in the church, from the appearance of those who always lead the meetings. The style of dress varies from one group to another, but again can communicate a whole series of messages: do visitors need to dress up or dress down to feel comfortable? Are the people who lead wearing what appears to be fancy dress to an outsider?

Thankfully we are seeing a shift in thinking about the use of buildings by churches. They are no longer seen by many as 'sanctuaries' in which only worship can take place. It is a fact of life that we need buildings for all sorts of purposes, but what we use, when we use them, and how, should be determined by what is most appropriate for the task in hand rather than by an Old Testament cultural approach.

We cannot avoid culture, nor should we try. It is important that we remember our own identity and reflect the backgrounds which are an integral part of our lives. We cannot hope to be relevant to all people, in every way, all of the time. It simply is not possible to hold in tension all culturally accessible forms of expression appropriate for every group. What we can do is make sure that cultural factors facilitate the communication of the gospel, and do not obstruct it.

A friend in Zambia has been writing to me at length over the last few months. In their church they are seeing many of the experiences that we have been going through here. The established churches have become rigid, formal and irrelevant. The charismatic movement has exploded onto the scene, bringing with it release and new life, and also tearing apart the 'old wineskins'. It is sad to think that in exporting the gospel, the British church has also sent its own culture, traditions, and ultimately its own problems.

It need not be this way. We are in the process of seeing tremendous changes in the nineties, in which the church is becoming more relevant to people inside and outside its membership. We are in the vanguard of a movement which is reaching men, young people and children who are traditionally lost to the church.

CHAPTER 7

UK CULTURE

A little while ago, I watched a television programme about advertising. The approach and ways of working in this area of business were quite new to me. I was fascinated as executives from different companies confidently asserted that they could predict which sort of product would sell in the nineties. They spoke of trends in society, swings in the aspirations and desires of individuals, and the way in which they could successfully target certain types of people. These commercial prophets had their fingers on the pulse of society and could work out a strategy to reach their intended mission field with details of a particular product.

Society is continually evolving. It expresses its life through culture which may shift also. I am not suggesting that the church should copy the goals or methods of the advertising companies, but I do believe that we have a lot to learn about strategy in mission. We need to accept the reality of where people are, not where they once were, or where we think they should be.

The family

During the last couple of generations, we have seen the pattern and make-up of the family shifting away from that of the nuclear. We know that over a third of all marriages will end in divorce. One-fifth of all the UK children alive in the last decade have experienced the splitting up of their parents, or will do so. Nearly one-third of all the children born are conceived outside marriage. As a result of this disruption to the traditional family picture, 10% of women are single mothers and 17% of all households in the UK are occupied by single parents. Interestingly, by contrast, the vast majority of the population are still in favour of the traditional family pattern. Inevitably, this brings tensions.

Family structures are increasingly fragmented, which reduces the support that can be gained. Parents may be more isolated and have less help to call upon. It may be difficult to get to meetings, they may have less time to talk, and be dealing with pressing emotional and financial issues. There may be no one else to turn to for advice, and they may have problems finding suitable accommodation on one or no income. There is often a need for counselling, networks of supportive friends, playschemes and nursery provision.

Although it is calculated that real disposable income has increased by 80% per person over the last twenty years, the gap between rich and poor has considerably widened. Women are always hit harder by unemployment, and since they make up the majority of single parents, money problems may be a very real issue. This may be compounded by media pressure particularly aimed at children and teenagers. More than half the young teenagers in the UK own at least one of these items—a television, camera or hi-fi.

Looking to the future, the profile of the family is shifting also. We have the lowest-ever fertility figure in Britain, 1.8 per woman. The Statistical Office comments, 'We think that this is probably the lowest fertility rate in Europe's entire history.' Between 1987 and 1995 the number in the 16–19 age group is expected to fall by 25%. However, 15% of the population are over 65. This upward shift in age distribution may mean that we have to re-evaluate evangelistic strategy. Clearly local factors play an important part. There are areas of London which consist largely of young single parents and their families, and others predominantly inhabited by much older people.

Race

I grew up in Southall, an area of West London. As a boy, I remember the first wave of Indian immigrants who were later to develop the area into one of the most densely Asian areas of Europe. Southall today is a remarkable place full of Indian shops, resplendent with the bright colours of sari fabric and the delicious smells of oriental spices. At that time, there was a tremendous amount of misunderstanding and hostility. Rumours were spread and people moved out. As a youngster, I could not see what the fuss was about. It is true that the young immigrants were mainly separated from the rest of the school for special language classes, but in the playground I could not see that these newcomers were really very different. This outlook was not shared by the churches in the area however, whose members often sold up and moved out. Many of the local Christians resented this new threat and retreated into more of a cultural siege mentality. Now the situation has changed, with Punjabi pastors and congregations, and a real attempt at cross-cultural mission.

There are over three million people of ethnic minorities in Britain, 5.5% of the total population. Nearly half have been born in the UK. Nearly half originate from the Indian subcontinent. The distribution throughout the British Isles is very variable, with 44% of ethnic groups in Greater London, and 14% in the West Midlands. In London, a recent survey showed that 127 different languages were spoken in the homes of the capital's children! Inner London has a quarter of its people drawn from ethnic groups. In Haringey, the borough in which we live, the figure is nearly a third, with sizeable minorities from the Tamil, Turkish, Greek, Kurdish and Somali communities amongst others. However, this picture is not universal. I once led a mission in South Devon during which a team took the local school assembly. The headmaster, in thanking us afterwards, paid special attention to an African team member, as most of the children had never seen anyone black before.

There are tremendous opportunities for mission and evangelism, and the possibility of modelling a cross-cultural identity which is largely unknown in society, where people from different racial backgrounds can find a safe place. This is especially significant as future population trends suggest rapid growth particularly within the Pakistani and Bangladeshi communities, still largely unreached by the gospel. There is a very young population structure within many ethnic groups—one out of three are under sixteen compared with one out of five of the white population. We are also seeing an upsurge in arrivals from Europe, East and West, both to study and to work in the UK.

Although there have been tremendous changes within British society, and our tolerance is far better than most of our European neighours, there is still much that can be done by the church. One in four Afro-Caribbeans describe Britain as 'very racist', with less than half of all respondents saying that the situation has improved over the last decade. If we do not respond, others will. According to one leading Muslim, 'This ingrained racism (of the English) is our lifeline. It brings many of our young people back to Islam.'

Religion

It is estimated that one in ten people attend church regularly in the UK. Up to half the population would claim some sort of church affiliation and two-thirds are sympathetic to Christian belief. Secularism has also grown and nearly one-third describe themselves as having 'no religion'. The majority of those who leave the church do so before they reach their mid-twenties. I have commented previously on church decline, but in recent years we have seen the growing strength of the 'charismatic evangelicals' whose effect has been to turn a sharp yearly decrease in the number of active Christian believers into a levelling-off. We are now at the start of what appears to be a definite trend upwards in church growth.

Seventy per cent of the population believe that the church should be involved in tackling locally identifiable problems such as loneliness, and the plight of the terminally ill, the elderly and the disabled. The church still has a place in popular culture, and this will be reinforced as Channel 4, amongst other media organisations, have taken the policy decision for the nineties to chart the progress of what they call the 'new Christian Fundamentalists'. However, we do need to recognise that the backdrop of society has changed. 'We have moved from where Christianity is culture to where Christianity is choice,' says the handbook *'Christian' England* (MARC Europe, 1991).

The other world religions practised in Britain constitute the following percentages of the population:

Muslim	2.5%
Sikh	0.8%
Hindu	0.7%
Jewish	0.6%
Buddhist	0.15%

Of course, some areas or groups will identify very strongly with a particular religion. In our area, there are many Jewish people; the Turkish, Kurdish and Bangladeshi communities have cultures linked strongly with Islam; Tamils tend to be from a Hindu background. We need to come up with strategies that will make a difference to these communities. As the church did not take the gospel to the world's doorstep, God has brought the world to the church's doorstep—a fantastic opportunity!

Sometimes people are intimidated by the apparent strength of adherence and devotion seen in other religious groups. We must remember that many Jews, for example, are not 'religious'—that is, they are only involved in high festivals. Indeed many are atheists or agnostics who see Judaism as culture alone. Sikhs are very open to other religions, and put great importance on respecting the beliefs of others. The first convert in my first church plant was a young Sikh man, and I well remember the respectful visits paid to us by his family elders. Hindus also are very welcoming to Christians.

Contrary to the popular view, the majority of Muslims in the UK are likely to be Muslim more by culture than by personal commitment. It makes a very strong link, but for many it still resembles the way in which a lot of British people would claim to be 'C of E' if asked their religious orientation. This is particularly true as the second and third generations of immigrant families seek to reconcile the culture of their parents with that of the society around them. This in itself can cause great distress as young people ask questions, but it is also a time of openness to the gospel.

Although some Christians seem quite paranoid about Islam and indeed Muslims, I believe there is far greater risk from the pervasive world views of agnostic materialism and pseudospiritual New Age. The British culture is one in which people do not take kindly to being told what to do and think. The only likely British converts to Islam are those who have the obsessive personality type which makes a good Jehovah's Witness. However, the militant Muslims will continue to evangelise hard, especially amongst disaffected ethnic groups, and on many campuses they are now the largest students' group. Their militancy also provokes problems though, with the students' unions asking the college authorities to ban the Islamic societies in some places.

On a personal level, I have always found Muslims more than happy to talk about Jesus, and we have an increasing number of converted Muslims in the fellowship. Nonetheless, they are adept at attracting media attention and infiltrating local prevailing cultures, aiming always to dominate rather than be assimilated by these cultures. To quote Lesslie Newbigin: 'In the twenty-first century, the main global alternative to Christianity will be Islam. Islam will not accept relegation to the private sector as

Christianity has in many societies—so tamely done. Islam, like Maoism, seeks to identify ultimate truth with actual political power.'

Summary

I have looked at three of the most important areas, but I am conscious that we have hardly touched other obvious subcultures such as the mentally ill, the disabled and gay groups. Each represent significant minorities of largely unreached people. Such smaller groups transcend ethnic considerations, but readily fit into identifiable groups with shared trends, ideas and behaviour patterns. At every stage, our appropriate desire to reach each of these groups must not be betrayed by our inappropriate beliefs about them or misplaced means of communication.

In Islington, it was found that although black people constituted 28% of the congregations, they were represented as 6% of the Deanery Synod. In the church, we must seek to reflect fully the community around us at every level, and not become trapped in a time warp or form a cultural ghetto.

CHAPTER 8

CROSSING THE DIVIDE

Sometimes when we consider people from our neighbourhood, especially those from a very different background, we feel overawed by how far they must come to embrace the gospel. There seem to be so many hurdles which they need to overcome, that we feel intimidated even before we start our evangelism!

Breaking down this process in our thinking and approach can be very helpful. In our attempts to see people come into the Kingdom, we can confuse outreach and evangelism. The words are often used interchangeably, but I believe that they refer to separate ends of a spectrum of activity. Outreach involves finding ways of getting to know people in the first place, making friends and building relationships. Evangelism involves the sharing of the gospel, ultimately leading to an encounter with Jesus.

Some Christians are very good at forming relationships within the fringe of a church or in the community, but are not often responsible for seeing those contacts become believers. They are good 'outreachers'. Others sit down next to one of those carefully cared-for contacts, and in a few minutes have introduced them to Christ! They are good 'evangelists' who can press through and have a gift for 'clinching the deal'.

To put it another way, outreach is seeing non-Christians become my friends; evangelism is seeing my friends become Christians. They are two aspects of the same process.

The problem for many Christians is that they no longer have good-quality relationships with people who do not share their beliefs. A good friend of mine shared recently that he no longer had regular contact with anyone outside his church. There were particular reasons for this, but even so, many of us need to know some non-Christians before we can hope to see them saved! This does not mean 'cold' evangelism such as street preaching and door visitation is of no value. However, research and experience show that the great majority of people become Christians as the result of friendship.

Developing a heart for the community

The last census reported that there were around 187,000 inhabitants in the London borough of Haringey. That is a bigger number than those who lived in the great city of Nineveh to which Jonah the reluctant prophet was sent. We need to remember that God's heart is just as much for the men, women and children who live in Haringey as it ever was for those who lived in Nineveh. We may not be as reluctant or judgemental as Jonah, but there is still a tremendous need for us to respond to God's call in reaching out. The individuals living around us are not 'the enemy', they just need saving. Outreach is the interface. The aim is to create a series of specialised points of contact appropriate to the people at whom we are aiming. It is at this stage that we can get to know them for their own sake, not simply as 'targets'. People deserve our interest and respect without conditions. From these contact points they can be filtered through to evangelistic meetings and strategies. There are a number of important points to remember in this process which I shall work through in the next few pages:

a) Pray for passion
If we are truly going to reach those around us, we need a passion which will allow devotion to God and service for others. In our personal walk with God, we become aware of the limitless love in His heart, and of His desire

to begin a relationship with those who do not know Him. Through His Spirit we are prepared to make changes and be flexible because of our passion for those who may be eternally lost.

b) Identify particular groups

We may need to research the area so that we know exactly who lives in the locality. This will involve an idea of the major ethnic groups, social conditions and family environment. It will perhaps give us an idea of a way into that section of the community. There is a church in a neighbouring borough which is at the heart of a large Japanese population. Having identified and researched that community, that church could then create contact points such as mother and toddler groups, language classes and communal meals through which friendship could grow between church members and the Japanese community.

Friends who are missionaries to Mongolia told me a salutary story. Until a few years ago, Mongolia had always been a country completely closed to the gospel. However, for many years the government have sent their best students to learn English at a major English university. These students then return to many of the senior positions in the country. The remarkable fact is that none of the local churches in the university town, or the Christian Union, seemed aware of the possibilities of outreach! As some Christians prayed for access to the distant Mongolian people, others missed the opportunity of reaching many of their future leaders while they were actually living in their own area!

c) Go where people are

It has always amazed me that most churches expect people to walk off the street into their meetings. I do not go to a golf club because I am not interested in golf. Why should we expect others to appear in church spontaneously when they do not think we are relevant? We have to earn the right to be heard, and one of the ways we do that is by identifying with local people.

Area congregations in our own church, the Rainbow, use a variety of 'user-friendly' venues. These include community centres, pubs and theatres. These are places where people either already meet, or feel quite safe when they do go there. We must be aware too that any of these chosen venues may put some off whilst attracting others. For example, the pub is not necessarily the best place to focus on children, old people, and those from Muslim backgrounds! Putting the church into the middle of an estate, as one of our area congregations has done, provokes questions and interest from all the residents, as well as giving a high profile and making a statement of integrity.

d) Start where people are

In outreach it is important to remember that most individuals will not share the same world view as ourselves. Their interests, ways of thinking, motivations and behavioural patterns may be markedly different. We should try and find out where they are mentally, and endeavour to build bridges across some common ground. It is not our aim to attack the particular mindsets that people bring with them, but rather to show them that we have something, or someone, who is better. In our meetings we aim to put across God's heart concerning an agenda which is important to us all. Subjects such as family life, sex and loneliness are accessible to all. The highly successful Pioneer initiative, Interface, which attracts hundreds of young people to fast-moving, magazine-style events, is a good example of, as Michael Green describes it, 'putting our message in their clothes'. Many people have to overcome their prejudices about church in order to come anywhere near the message. For some we need to distinguish between Christianity and a British culture from which they feel alienated.

e) Identify particular needs

I was recently asked to see a middle-aged man from Trinidad whose marriage was in the process of breaking up. He came from a Muslim background but was open to what I had to say. In addressing the focus of his problems, the impending divorce and his emotional turmoil, I started at his point of need. It rapidly became possible to invite him to pray and read Psalms in order to allay his anxiety. Soon he was broadening his support network by attending meetings and getting to know other people in the fellowship. Within a few weeks he had committed his life to Christ. Had I weighed in straightaway with his need for salvation, ignoring what he believed to be relevant, we would soon have parted company.

This is also true in the local church as a whole. Another of our area congregations have started CATs—Community Action Teams. The fellowship are divided into teams to work on programmes that address needs expressed by the local community. We are fortunate in making use of a school building which is surplus to the council's requirements. In it we run a youth club, children's club, play group, advice centre, coffee mornings, aerobics class, as well as allowing activities such as the local Tenants' Association meeting to take place. We realise that we have to take a longer-term view before acquaintance becomes friendship, but we have created a large 'fringe' to the church into which the outreachers and evangelists can work. Each church should grow a healthy fringe!

f) Find people of peace

All the time we are looking for 'the men of peace' (Luke 10:6), those people who will open up their families, friends, contacts and homes to us. In this way, we gain access to communities which may otherwise be closed to us. The reason why the Rainbow has such a strong Tamil connection, having planted two Tamil-speaking congregations in London and seven abroad is because of these 'people of peace'—individuals who opened up access to relatives and friends here and overseas, allowing the good news to be taken from house to house because of a trustworthy introduction and their recommendation. This principle is essential in gaining access geographically to, say, an estate, street or tower block, as to a particular group, for instance, to students or an ethnic group. It is important to pray for these breakthrough people who can make the connections and have the credibility. For two years, I have prayed specifically for 'people of peace' who can open up doorways into the Greek and Turkish communities.

g) Don't exclude the supernatural

Do not be afraid to expose people, even at the outreach stage, to the supernatural. We regularly hold healing and prophecy meetings aimed at outsiders—and they come! We encourage praying for individuals in evangelism, including out on the street. There is so much emphasis in the media on the supernatural, and on New Age thought, that many have no problem at all in talking along those lines. There are those who will not give you the time of day if you start sharing the gospel, but if you offer to pray for someone in their house who is sick, they will listen. Miracles cross cultural boundaries!

h) Be available

We should be accessible to those we reach out to in terms of time and commitment. The world is full of false promises—we can show that in the Kingdom life is of a different quality. We find ourselves visiting someone who is housebound or collecting the groceries. We may have to make ourselves available by learning another language, allowing people to break into our privacy by dropping in without an appointment, or building flexibility into our work and church arrangements. We can be provoked to extend very practical help to those who may be homeless. We may even be challenged to move into an area or extend our households. Our tightly channelled views of being available may not create the access points that others look for. We learn to witness through works, words and wonders.

My wife, Jean, is superb at spending time with Jehovah's Witnesses. For most of us, they have a habit of turning up when we are too busy to fetch our Bibles and talk. Jean just invites them in and gets chatting. She shows them a regard and acceptance which they never experience within the movement. One lady used to bring a succession of Witness friends to meet her, so that they could listen to her testimony! Jean made herself available in time and friendliness.

Heterogenous vs. homogeneous

A homogeneous group of people are those who share a similar background and culture. Generally speaking, it is easier to reach out to a homogeneous group. It is possible to concentrate resources in a single-minded way. Those reached will feel less vulnerable and can retain their identity. When there are believers established within that group, they are more able to communicate with their peers. This is a good and helpful principle for the initial breakthrough, but if adhered to, will cause isolation from the rest of the community.

I was interested to hear one of the leaders of the so-called 'black churches' describe the problems that they are now experiencing. For long enough, their homogeneity within well-defined cultural groups was their strength. Now they realise that they are dealing with second and third generations of Afro-Caribbeans who do not share the same cultural heritage as their parents. They also want to impact a largely white society. To achieve these aims, their approach has to become less homogeneous.

However, we are trying this strategy in student outreach, particularly to those of Chinese and Muslim origin. We are able to use appropriate language resources, building up a group identity, and introduce outreachers from a similar background. As a result, we have established evangelistic Bible studies involving

Iranian, Turkish, Kurdish and Chinese students. We are hoping not only to see these students respond to Jesus, as some already have, but to act as a bridge into local ethnic populations with whom they are homogeneous. In time, some may develop a heart for evangelising and church planting back into their nations of origin. By influencing them, we may impact many unreached parts of the world!

Summary

In outreach, we hope to form networks of relationships in a variety of ways and on different levels, which criss-cross communities with relevant and appropriate strategies. There is no point in simply expecting people to adapt to our own culture, church or otherwise. We can hope to build a series of specialised access points which can in turn introduce our new friends to appropriate evangelism.

CHAPTER 9

SEIZING THE TIME

Working with students has made me realise that we should make the most of the time and the opportunities while they exist. There may be a 'window of opportunity' which is only open for a given season. During this, people are accessible to an encounter with Jesus, and we should be ready to provide the invitation. It is at this stage that we raid our outreach fringe and challenge with relevant evangelism.

However, if we hope to present our friends with the truth of God, we need to make sure that our church is ready to cross cultural barriers, to make way for newcomers of a different background, and that it is a demonstration of the King and the Kingdom. We cannot hope to make a longlasting impact unless what we do is based in a community where there is reality in worship and fellowship. The aim in at least some of our church meetings is to create a 'safe place for a dangerous message'—where in a variety of ways we seek to express the gospel in such a way that outsiders can taste and learn, but can still feel secure.

Seeker services

A lot of attention has been given recently to the approach of one of the fastest-growing churches in the USA, Willow Creek, on the edge of Chicago. Their desire, as the main leader, Bill Hybels, puts it, is to 'create a church for the unchurched'. They do not neglect the need for pastoral care and Bible teaching, but their major emphasis is on providing culturally relevant, top-quality, high-profile evangelism. Although their approach could not be transplanted wholesale into another area or society, the underlying principle can, and has indeed been used to good effect by other groups, including some in the UK.

We have used a concept called Kaleidoscope, which involved putting together a mixture of drama, music, dance and art to express the heart of God on a number of contemporary issues. These included family, prejudice, sex and education, all of which are of importance to the majority of unreached people. At two performances, over five hundred came, many from a totally unchurched background. One of them, a well-known composer for the BBC and a member of the BAFTA awards jury, said that he had not seen anything so fresh and exciting for over twenty years. Another guest, a rock promoter who has since come into the church, described it as 'like the sixties but without the sex'!

These were large-scale events which needed over seventy people to stage. However, it is possible to produce similar ideas on a smaller level more frequently. 'Big Issues' are monthly meetings in our regular service slots which address themes creatively and sensitively, but powerfully. These have included eating disorders, addictions and healing. It is then possible to invite people to these meetings knowing that as much as possible will be done to incorporate the visitors.

Put the needs of outsiders first

This has to be one of the most significant factors to be considered, and for many churches it would determine a radical shift in what takes place in certain meetings.

- *Good publicity is essential.* It should be of a high quality, suitable for the target group, and may even include more than one language. There is a need to create an attractive image, distinct from that given by the usual shoddy photocopied sheets pushed through the door. Advertisers say that the single most important factor is the meaningfulness of the message presented.

- The *setting* should be chosen with care. This involves the venue and the framework. One memorable and successful evening was a curry night in a school building using an evangelistic conjuror! Many people will only relax in a situation of friendly anonymity.
- *Good quality presentation* helps people take the message seriously. This will involve teamwork, commitment, time, planning, money and rehearsal, but the results make it all worthwhile. A series of these fast-moving events within a hostel is reaping good contacts with overseas students, including many Muslims.
- Communication should be *relevant*. This applies not only to the subjects, but also to the need to avoid 'in-jokes', unnecessary announcements, jargon and offensive argument. It should never be patronising or cause embarrassment. The programme and those taking part will need introduction and explanation. Tough questions should be faced, and we should present evidence and reasons for our views, as well as showing whether what we are saying works in practice. I know of one church on the edge of South London working in a gypsy community. They are learning ways of communicating with a mainly illiterate audience.
- Content should somehow focus on, or lead back to, *Jesus and the resurrection*. All that we uniquely have to offer is based on these. Our biblical concept of God and humanity is applied to the secular experience of our audience, using the common ground of life. We begin where they are, and provoke them tenderly to consider the value of what is being communicated. We

seek to get people intrigued, without making any assumptions, and above all fascinated by Jesus. I do not cease to be amazed at how struck many people are when they hear about Jesus for the first time. Immediately the sight of Kurdish and Iranian students reading about Jesus in their own Bibles springs to mind, or the description given by a lecturer from Beijing, a veteran of Tiananmen Square, of the first time he had heard about Easter.

- In all that we do, we remember we are dealing with *friends, not projects.* We respect their integrity and cultural forms, their right to choose, and we relinquish our right to be defensive. To quote Bill Hybels, 'Lost people matter to God, therefore they matter to you.'

Count the cost

This will be inevitable as we make the needs of the unchurched our priority. As someone once said, 'The church is the only organisation on earth that exists for those who are not yet its members.' We may have to alter our cherished timetables, programmes and presentation. The emphasis on praise and worship or teaching about the saints might give way at some of our meetings to accommodating those who seek the Jesus we adore. Undoubtedly we will find that money, time and personnel are set aside to enable our vision to reach out.

There are sometimes important aids which facilitate the goals. Finding scriptures and booklets in appropriate languages, buying videos, paying for speakers with particular expertise can all be useful. Making sure that key people are trained, equipped and released does not come cheaply. Even the provision of interpreters for a specific group or the installation of a loop system to help the hard of hearing may be thought advantageous.

All the time we are aiming to ask and provoke questions about belief. As a result, some may be called to involve themselves very closely with the system they seek to replace, as in taking the time to learn the Qur'an or reading copies of the *Watchtower*. We may spend hours listening and watching, trying to understand the Jewish approach to life or why homosexuals feel alienated from the church. Each time we make the effort to communicate with another people group we are punching holes in the enemy's strategy.

Often there is a spiritual battle which needs to be recognised. The enemy knows that every time a member of a previously unreached people group gets saved, it is another step nearer to his ultimate defeat. It is no surprise then, that when we attempt to cross cultures we encounter overt and subtle opposition. One high-profile event involving churches from varied ethnic backgrounds was nearly stopped by the local council who had hired us the hall. This was due to misunderstandings fuelled by the local press.

The cost to be borne involves praying for breakthrough and spiritual warfare. We may find ourselves called to fasting and intercession. There may be a need to protect new disciples, and in some cases to compensate for the family and social networks which their conversion has cost them. We need to recognise how significant the conversion of certain individuals can be in terms of their representing a particular people group. For instance, if we are in the process of evangelising someone whose nation has no known church, then we must anticipate an intense spiritual struggle.

Expose to the heart of God

Although we do not want to shock or scare our friends in the process, we should want to show them the reality of a big God who not only cares, but has the power to show that He cares. I have longed for churches to be known as dangerous places, in the sense that people know that if they go into the meetings, they will not come out the same! Could the government issue a health warning about our church, saying that those who enter do so at the risk of eternal change?

Increasingly, the practice of the spiritual gifts, especially prophecy and healing, are seen to be in the context of touching the unbeliever. I can remember speaking prophetic words into the life of a young girl in the old Czechoslovakia, the daughter of a senior Communist army officer. It was only halfway through that I realised she was not a Christian! Two days later, largely as a result of the words she had received, she committed herself to God. Let us give the Holy Spirit the space to do what only He can do!

The radical edge

As we try to make ourselves culturally relevant, and see people exposed to the heart of God, there will be untidy edges and uncomfortable moments. God often seems to move in 'sanctified chaos'! He is actually more comfortable with the grey, blurred areas than we are. This is reality, rather than a clean-cut, black and white imitation that is sometimes projected by the church.

Not far from where I live is the church building which holds the largest congregation in the borough. It is a Greek Orthodox cathedral. Some months ago, I asked one of the priests about the size of the congregation. With obvious pride, he told me that in an average week ten thousand people attended the various services! Incidentally, it was interesting to note that even they complain about their offerings! I may admire their ability to have regular contact with so many, but of course it is totally regulated by set form and tradition, and is completely restricted to a single language and culture. I mention this not to dismiss such churches out of hand, but to point to a contrast.

In a gloriously multicultural society such as ours, the

key to the future is surely flexibility. This will enable us to manoeuvre into a position where we can take advantage of God-given opportunities, to determine our programme according to need, and to live with the consequent untidiness.

> There are lively growing churches which are finding new ways to express God's love to their communities. This may mean changing some of the church's meetings to appeal to non-Christians, rather than always expecting non-Christians to adapt to the culture of the church.
>
> (Ruth March, in *LandMARC,* Spring '92)

CHAPTER 10

INTEGRATED CHURCH

Although I have spoken of the value of dealing with homogeneous groups in outreach, our ultimate goal is something quite different. To keep Christians in cultural boxes would simply perpetuate those divisions. When we all mix together irrespective of our backgrounds we find a context in which we can recognise and deal with our deep-seated prejudices. There will always be a place for home groups or congregations which retain a distinctive cultural flavour, or have their meeting in certain languages. These will help to maintain identity and facilitate evangelism amongst people sharing the same characteristics. However, when these home groups or congregations come together in celebration, they all merge together in a single integrated church.

A mainly 'black' church is just as limiting as one which is mainly 'white'. The great test of maturity and intention is whether fellowships originating out of one group can eventually break out, making room for others. This test faces the Tamil congregations in France and Switzerland, working mainly amongst refugees. Now they are starting to develop a heart for the surrounding indigenous population, and are having meetings simultaneously in Tamil and French or German.

We must remember too that no single group, background or tradition has a monopoly on Christ. We can learn from one another, and each has an important distinctive role within the Body. The exuberant creativity which God has shown in nature is nowhere better displayed than in the variety of humans with whom He has chosen to populate the earth. At Pioneer conferences, signing for the deaf has become a significant feature. Many of us who do not share such a disability get excited at the visually uninhibited expression of worship which communicates using the hands and body. As we are open to one another, even what might appear to be our points of weakness can inspire someone else.

East London has a long history of racial tension, sometimes erupting into violence. Recently we have seen the re-emergence of political extremism and agitation. We organised an event in Bethnal Green called 'Standing Together' in which local Christians of several fellowships joined together in united worship and prayerful solidarity. This was no protest meeting, but rather the opportunity to revel together in Jesus. The other organising church has a large number of people mainly originating from Ghana. Alongside the contemporary songs of Noel Richards were the complex rhythms of African drums, the 'charismatic shuffle' joining with swaying dances involving the waving of flags and hankies! Hundreds of men, women and children distinctive in brightly coloured clothes met and appreciated one another. We prayed together, joined hands, embraced, and had one heaven of a praise party!

Every time we do something like this, it is a demonstration to a fractured society of a better way, God's way. Where the world fails, the church must act in harmony. Meetings such as these become a prophetic declaration and demonstration of the heart of the King and the rule of the Kingdom. It is a foretaste of what is to come, but experienced in the here and now.

Another exciting development in our generation is the large number of children who have parents from two cultures. Traditionally society has viewed this as a problem, with anxieties about whether such families will be 'at home' within one group or another. This may be a real problem in certain circumstances. However, in a multiracial society, I see this as a real strength. This bringing together of two different backgrounds, races and languages into one home, possibly distilled into one child, is in itself a prophetic demonstration to the world. It shows how barriers can be overcome, and cultures can unite without collision. One set of neighbours is a family consisting of a Turkish father, a Polish mother, and children who speak Turkish, Polish and English! If anyone wanted to look for such a combination of learned languages, it would be difficult to find! Some friends of my children speak French, Armenian and English, again because of their parents! God is raising up a generation of children who are not only a prophetic demonstration, but could be a key in unlocking areas of the world through multilingual, cross-cultural evangelism! Potentially they can not only bridge the divide between separated groups in our society, but also move freely across the larger national and language barriers. If we aim to reach the world in one generation, it is precisely the emergence of an army of such people which will facilitate the process.

We may also see further developments in our understanding of family. Instead of closing out the world when we shut our front doors, we may bring the world in with us. Our immediate neighbours are Jewish on one side, and Polish Catholic and Turkish Muslim on the other. Across the street are flats housing African and Turkish refugees. Inside the house are my wife and myself, our three children, and three single adults from widely varying backgrounds. Depending on where we live and our particular circumstances, the potential for exploring and intergrating with other cultures can be immense. Many others within the church have an extended view of household, and an openness to neighbours and friends. They are ready to parent the unparented and befriend the friendless. When this is duplicated many times over, we begin to see the results of friendship turning into commitment, and the church reflecting more closely all the fragments of society, but in a way which allows for integration. The world is looking for someone to get it right. If the church cannot model integration, no one else can.

God is waiting for the church to reach into every people group, so that the bride will be complete in her purity. God teaches many spiritual truths within the natural, physical realm. The totality of perfect light is made up of the different colours of the visible spectrum. They exist within it but are indistinguishable when they merge together. Each colour has its own identity within the whole, but unites to gain a nature which is even more splendid. When we contemplate the age to come, we know from scripture that every people group will be distinctively represented. The ultimate expression of praise and worship is when we join together united as the one body before Jesus.

As the single beam cuts through the air
Rainbow colours scatter everywhere
Each portrays its own identity
Merging back in perfect synchrony

Let your pure light always shine through me
With the radiance of eternity
May it take the colour of my soul
Changing others as it makes me whole

RECOMMENDED READING

Mohabir, Philip, *World Within Reach* (Hodder and Stoughton, 1992)

Montgomery, Jim, *Dawn 2000: 7 million churches to go* (William Carey Library, 1989)

Johnstone, Patrick, *Operation World* (OM Publishing, 1993)

Brierley, Peter, *'Christian' England : Results of the English Church Census* (MARC Europe, 1991)

THE POWER TO PERSUADE

The Media and the Church

Cleland Thom

How does your community regard your church? What image does it present? A relic from the past? A semicredible bunch of weirdos? Or a group of caring people keen to spread God's love in today's world?

Churches cannot afford to ignore the fact that newspapers are among the primary shapers of opinion these days. It's easy to sit back and moan about bad—or no—publicity, but Christians must act positively to inform the press of their activities, make sure the message is the one they want the public to read, and learn how to use the influence of the media to advance God's kingdom on earth. We must be bearers of good news, and thus begin to create a climate in which our evangelistic activities will be better received.

This is a thoroughly practical *Perspective* which states the case for having a church with a high media profile, and then offers a clear guide to how to go about it, with no cost and little risk. You will find a mine of information and helpful advice about setting up a publicity structure, writing letters and press releases, producing church literature, using the press for evangelism, how to complain, using advertising and many other topics, all based on the author's practical experience in journalism.